MARRAKE

THE CITY AT A GLA

Ben Youssef Mosque
After Koutoubia (see p010), t
mosque is the second tallest
It's named after the Almoravi
rebuilt several times by succeeding dynasties.
Its wooden crown watches over the Ben
Youssef Medersa, or Koranic school (see p070).
Off Rue Souk El Khemis

Musée de Marrakech
Part of the lure of this museum, which
exhibits Moroccan artefacts and crafts, is the
building itself: the 19th-century Dar Menebhi,
a beautifully restored Andalusian-style palace.
Place Ben Youssef, T 0 524 441 893

Sidi Ben Salah Zaouia
Distinguished by its distinctive 14th-century
minaret, this *zaouia* (sanctuary) was built
by the Marinids, the Berber tribe that
followed hot on the heels of the Almohads
and claimed the city in 1269.
Rue Ba Hmad

Sidi Bel Abbès Zaouia
Marrakech's patron saint lends his name to
a tranquil, less touristy quarter in the north
of the medina. His shrine is set within an
impressive *zaouia* and garden complex.
Jnane Sidi Bel Abbès

Souk El Khemis
For the patient shopper, this is the most
interesting souk. All sorts of antiques,
bric-a-brac and curios are hawked in the
shops and daily outdoor market.
Off Route des Remparts

INTRODUCTION
THE CHANGING FACE OF THE URBAN SCENE

'It's the most lovely spot in the whole world,' said Churchill to Franklin D Roosevelt about Marrakech in 1943. Since its founding in the 11th century, the Red City has seduced visitors, from the architects and artisans who built its mosques and palaces, to the bohemians who rode the Marrakech Express at full throttle in the 1960s and 1970s. Lately, the city has, perhaps, become a victim of its own success, invaded by e-ticket tourists in search of some winter sun and instant escapism. This is quick-fix Marrakech, and one that is more than happy to offer up its beguiling souks and stucco wonders to the masses. Recently, though, to counterbalance the hedonistic allure, there's been a drive to promote the city as a cultural destination and a place for artistic exchange and debate within Morocco. The local contemporary art and design scenes are burgeoning, and the number of young Marrakechis creating their own businesses, from *boîtes* to boutiques, is on the rise.

Since the French arrived in 1912, Marrakech has balanced the ancient and the modern. Arguably, this is what makes it so appealing. If Morocco is the most liberal Arab country, Marrakech is its *ne plus ultra*. Another factor is glamour. The city has some of the most luxurious and romantic accommodation in the world, in one of the prettiest settings. Orientalist fantasy palace, intimate riad, impeccable five-star resort – it's all here. Classic Marrakech will always dazzle, but it has a fresh, 21st-century face too.

ESSENTIAL INFO

FACTS, FIGURES AND USEFUL ADDRESSES

TOURIST OFFICE
Office National Marocain du Tourisme
Place Abdel Moumen
Avenue Mohammed V
T 0 524 436 131
www.visitmorocco.com

TRANSPORT
Car hire
Avis
T 0 524 432 525
Hertz
T 0 524 439 984
Taxis
Petits taxis (small khaki-coloured Fiats,
Simcas or similar) can be flagged down
in the street. *Grands taxis* (larger cars,
normally Mercedes) are available
for longer distances and can be hired
at the railway station, most of the larger
hotels and cab ranks across the city

EMERGENCY SERVICES
Ambulance/Fire
T 15
Police
T 19
Late-night pharmacy
Pharmacie Centrale
166 avenue Mohammed V
T 0 524 430 158

CONSULATES
British Honorary Consulate
55 boulevard Zerktouni
T 0 537 633 333
www.ukinmorocco.fco.gov.uk
US Consulate General
8 avenue Moulay Youssef
Casablanca
T 0 522 264 550
morocco.usembassy.gov

POSTAL SERVICES
Post office
Place du 16 Novembre/
Avenue Mohammed V
Shipping
UPS
T 0 663 010 719
www.ups.com

BOOKS
Arabesques: Decorative Art in Morocco
by Jean-Marc Castera, Françoise Peuriot
and Philippe Ploquin (ACR Edition)
The Berbers by Michael Brett and
Elizabeth Fentress (Wiley-Blackwell)
**Marrakech: Living on the Edge of the
Desert** by Massimo Listri and Daniel Rey
(Images Publishing Group)

WEBSITE
News
www.emarrakech.info

EVENTS
Marrakech Art Fair
www.marrakechartfair.com
Marrakech Biennale
www.marrakechbiennale.org
Marrakech International Film Festival
www.festivalmarrakech.info

COST OF LIVING
Taxi from Menara Airport to city centre
120 dirhams
Cappuccino
28 dirhams
Packet of cigarettes
30 dirhams
Daily newspaper
4 dirhams
Bottle of champagne
1,100 dirhams

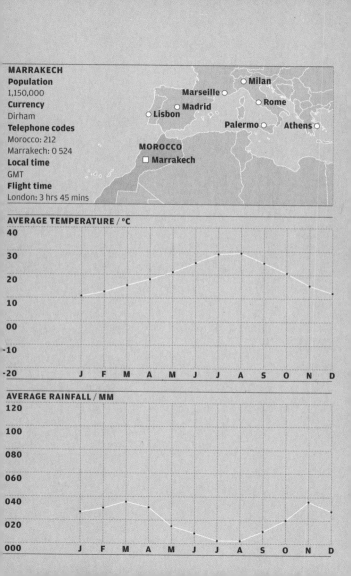

MARRAKECH
Population
1,150,000
Currency
Dirham
Telephone codes
Morocco: 212
Marrakech: 0 524
Local time
GMT
Flight time
London: 3 hrs 45 mins

Milan
Marseille
Madrid
Rome
Lisbon
Palermo
Athens

MOROCCO
Marrakech

AVERAGE TEMPERATURE / °C

	40												
30													
20													
10													
00													
-10													
-20	J	F	M	A	M	J	J	A	S	O	N	D	

AVERAGE RAINFALL / MM

120													
100													
080													
060													
040													
020													
000	J	F	M	A	M	J	J	A	S	O	N	D	

NEIGHBOURHOODS

THE AREAS YOU NEED TO KNOW AND WHY

To help you navigate the city, we've chosen the most interesting districts (see below and the map inside the back cover) and colour-coded our featured venues, according to their location; those venues that are outside these areas are not coloured.

SOUTH MEDINA

Shaped like an arrowhead, Marrakech's medina is one of Africa's largest. Frenetic and wholly stimulating, the southern half is the busiest part. Enter via the boulevard that stems from Koutoubia Mosque (see p010) and use Place Jemaa El Fna as your reference point. Taxis are barred from the core and from the square after dark; pick one up at one of the gates. La Mamounia (see p030) offers respite from the mayhem.

PALMERAIE

Legend has it this oasis was established in the 11th century by Youssef Ibn Tachfine, founder of Marrakech. Having made camp here, the sultan's servants spat out date seeds, thus planting the 200,000 or so palms growing in the area. Although much of the investment in luxury properties is now focused around Route de l'Ourika and Route d'Amizmiz, the Palmeraie still boasts some of the city's most appealing retreats, such as Dar Sabra (see p024).

NORTH MEDINA

The heart of the old city is where most of the big tourist attractions lie: the souks, Ben Youssef complex (see p068) and Musée de Marrakech (Place Ben Youssef, T 0 524 441 893). Less well trodden is the northern tip, where you'll spy workshops, bakeries, women on their way to the hammam, and other glimpses of urban life in an archaic setting. The market held around Souk El Khemis is worth a trawl.

HIVERNAGE

This leafy district of the new town is where the embassies of the French Protectorate and its officials set up home. Many of their descendants still live here, side by side with green spaces including the Menara Gardens (see p014). Those who know Hivernage of old would barely recognise it today, due to the number of trendy hotels and nightspots, such as Mooï (see p044) and Djellabar (see p060), popping up.

MELLAH/KASBAH

At the 'base' of the arrowhead is the most ancient part of Marrakech, the Kasbah, and the former Jewish quarter of the Mellah. Stay at Villa Makassar (see p026) and visit the remarkable Saadian Tombs (see p065) and magnificent rambling ruin of Palais El Badi (see p066). The architecture of the Mellah is distinct, its Spanish hanging balconies and colourful facades a legacy of the Moors and Sephardic Jews who fled the Inquisition.

GUÉLIZ

The French Protectorate was described as 'soft colonialism': its urban planning aimed to create a homogeneous whole between the new town and the medina. The *ville nouvelle*'s art deco glory days have passed, but the district is buzzing once again. Stroll along its wide avenues, visiting the streetside cafés and shops. Venues like L'Avenue (see p038) and Azar (see p058) have injected new vigour into the nightlife.

LANDMARKS
THE SHAPE OF THE CITY SKYLINE

In the labyrinth of medieval Marrakech, defining landmarks are hard to identify. One exception is Koutoubia Mosque (overleaf), whose minaret dominates the skyline and acts as a gateway to the old city's rambling morphology. The medina itself is ringed by 10km of ramparts (see p012), with ornamental entrances (*babs*) that give their names to its neighbourhoods and hubs. The focal point is Place Jemaa El Fna, the huge square that you'll return to again and again as you navigate this part of town; at night, it's a spectacle you should view at least once. From here, the souks lie to the north, and the Saadian Tombs (see p065) and Palais El Badi (see p066) to the south. Both are within easy walking distance.

The tranquil Menara Gardens (see p014), about 3km from the centre, are a world away from the medina. Journey through Hivernage and the landscape changes quickly from leafy urban streets lined with modern apartment blocks to vast olive groves. Head north into Guéliz, the heart of the *ville nouvelle*, and the scenery shifts again – Jardin Majorelle (see p034) is a reminder of the once-gracious cityscape of the French Protectorate. Sadly, most of Marrakech's art deco architecture is gone, with the exception of legendary grande dame, the 1923 La Mamounia (see p030). Perhaps the city's best-loved landmark, its dusky pink edifice and famous gardens now impress again thanks to a major restoration. *For full addresses, see Resources.*

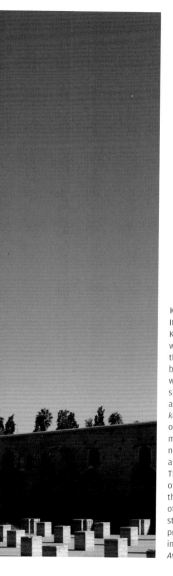

Koutoubia Mosque

It was the Almohads who completed Koutoubia's 69m minaret in 1189. And this was their second chance to get it right; the first minaret had to be torn down because its orientation towards Mecca was askew. Koutoubia was built on the site of an existing Almoravid mosque, and its name derives from the Arabic word *koutoubiyyin* (librarian) – bookstalls were once set up around its base. As with the majority of mosques in the Arab world, non-Muslims are barred from entry and will have to imagine the interior. The minaret has six rooms, one on top of the other, and the exterior features the horseshoe-shaped arches typical of the Andalusian-influenced Almohad style. Visit during one of the five daily prayer sessions, when the faithful file in from the surrounding gardens.
Avenue Mohammed V

Ramparts

Remarkably intact, the mud-and-lime wall enclosing the medina has borne witness to numerous sieges (the city was conquered by various colonising powers before it came under French rule in 1912). Of its main gates, Bab Agnaou and Bab Er Rob are the most interesting. Route des Remparts, running along the medina's eastern flank, is the best place to appreciate the wall's expanse.

Menara Gardens
Echoes of these lovely 12th-century gardens can be glimpsed throughout Marrakech. The pool at La Mamounia (see p030) was inspired by Menara's central reservoir, and its pioneering irrigation system, responsible for watering what are some of the oldest gardens in Morocco, has been replicated across the country and in Spain. Menara was the vision of Almohad ruler Abd Al-Mu'min, who wanted to provide his citizens with a manmade oasis around which they could grow crops and escape the heat. With the Atlas mountains forming a spectacular backdrop, the gardens have been a popular (and romantic) retreat for Marrakechis ever since. The focal point is a 19th-century pavilion (right), which replaced an earlier 16th-century structure built by the Saadians.
Avenue de la Ménara

HOTELS

WHERE TO STAY AND WHICH ROOMS TO BOOK

Marrakech has a dizzying array of accommodation, and the riad fever that has gripped the city for almost two decades rages on. Riads (or dars in their smaller form) are traditional Moroccan houses set around a courtyard. Over the years, they've been bought by foreigners for the price of a parking space back home and turned into *maisons d'hôte*. While most provide all the boutique-hotel trimmings, it pays to be choosy. A *zellige*-tiled bathroom will do little to compensate for bad lighting and low water pressure.

While recession bites elsewhere, luxury openings in Marrakech continue apace, with international brands, such as Four Seasons (1 avenue de la Ménara, T 0 524 359 200), streaming in. Where you stay is key. The medina will give you a taste of the old city, with its *djellaba*-clad street sellers and dusty zigzag alleys. Among the best-designed properties here is Riad Joya (see p021). Guéliz and Hivernage are newly buzzy and the savvy are staying at La Renaissance (89 boulevard Zerktouni, T 0 524 337 777), Mooï, which has a sleek club (see p044), and Pearl (Avenue Echouhada, T 0 524 424 100), a Jacques Garcia project. For more secluded surroundings, opt for the Palmeraie and the discreet Dar Sabra (see p024). South of the medina, the Raymond Morel-designed César Hôtel (Route de l'Ourika, T 0 524 369 900) has an upbeat feel. For private rentals, look no further than Habibi Homes (T 011 409 984). *For full addresses and room rates, see Resources.*

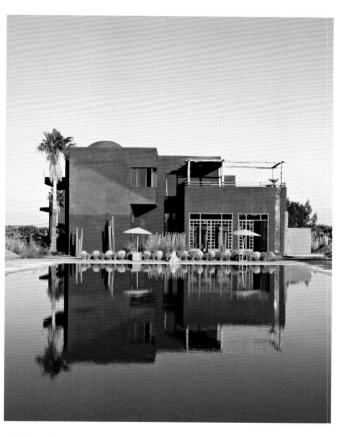

Fellah Hotel

An antidote to the hectic city, this 2011 property exudes tranquillity. It adjoins and helps fund the non-profit Dar Al-Ma'mûn arts centre, which was launched in 2010 with the aim of offering artists' residencies and cultural resources. Houria Afoufou, who co-owns the hotel with husband Redha Moali, devised the interiors: a modish mix of local crafts (rugs and leatherwork), vintage items and bespoke furniture. The accommodation comprises 10 villas, housing 69 rooms, such as the chic Suite 103 (overleaf). Chill out by the scenic pool (above) and relax in the knowledge that there's no need to drive 20 minutes into town each night. The restaurant is great, and the Salon Mahler bar is fast becoming a meeting point for Marrakechi creatives. *Route de l'Ourika km13, T 0 525 065 000, www.fellah-hotel.com/www.dam-arts.org*

Riad Tarabel

The mood is unmistakably Gallic at this riad owned by Frenchman Léonard Degoy. Taking oil paintings from a family castle in the village of Tarabel near Toulouse and antiques trawled from the fleamarkets of Paris and Marrakech, Degoy and his wife, Rose, have created a sophisticated medina retreat. Designer Romain Michel-Ménière advised on the original renovation and a recent extension increased the number of suites to seven; a courtyard pool and garden were also added. The Palmeraie Suite (above) and upstairs salon are typical of Tarabel's signature style, and there's a cosy screening room with plush sofas and a fireplace for colder days. The food, a melange of French and Moroccan cuisine, is prepared with similar Gallic panache.
8 Derb Sraghna, Dar El Bacha,
T 0 524 391 706, www.riadtarabel.com

Riad Joya

Elegance is the quality that Umberto Branchini Maria has brought to this riad in the medina's Mouassine quarter. In the interior architecture and seven suites, the Italian art director nods to the cultures that have inhabited Morocco, from the Romans to the Arabs. Doric travertine columns and cedar *moucharabieh* are key elements of the courtyard, while the rooms feature *tadelakt*, striped in the case of Dar Arabe (above), natural linens, silk, velvet and bronze, as well as raw wooden furniture. It all makes for a sumptuous but modern mix, thanks to the designer's light touch. The bathrooms, with their fabulous showers, are among the best we've come across in Marrakech. Joya's staff are delightful and the delicate food is a treat. *Hay Moussaine, Derb al Hammam 26-27, T 0 524 391 624, www.riadjoya.com*

Royal Mansour

Flawless craftsmanship, evident from the moment you step in the lobby (right), makes for a thrilling visual experience at the Royal Mansour, a palatial property backed by King Mohammed VI. Vast in scale, it's intended to resemble an entire medina, with walled grounds including 53 traditionally styled riads, ranging from one- to four-bedroom. It's hard not to be overawed by the sheer ambition of the project, and the attention to detail achieved by the craftsmen and Paris-based firm 3BIS, which created the interiors. Although given the jaw-dropping prices, this is accommodation that will be out of reach for most. More accessible are the spa (see p089), the dining – which includes Moroccan and French haute cuisine restaurants overseen by lauded chef Yannick Alléno – and the three bars. *Rue Abou Abbas El Sebti, T 0 529 808 080, www.royalmansour.com*

Dar Sabra

Originally his own getaway, the Palmeraie villa of French art enthusiast François Chapoutot was inspired by the work of late Mexican architect Ricardo Legorreta. In 2010, Chapoutot opened it as a hotel, working with architect Réda Amalou of French practice AW2 and designing the interiors himself. Expanded since its launch, Dar Sabra now has 10 rooms in the main house, eight in a new wing, including Solorzano (opposite), and a two-bedroom villa with a private pool and olive-grove gardens. Chapoutot's art collection undoubtedly enhances a stay here. Works range from a group of Senegalese marriage spears to stone sculptures by Japanese artist Satoru Sato. There are five pools in total and a bar/restaurant (above), as well as ample living rooms and a library in the main house.
Douar Abbiad, T 0 524 329 172, www.darsabra.com

Villa Makassar

Fouad Graidia spent five years restoring and embellishing two houses in the Kasbah, turning one into this handsome hotel in 2011. Inside, he has displayed the collection of art deco and modernist furniture and objects that he's been amassing since 1998. The library, for example, features Bauhaus onyx (similar to that which hung on the wall of the Mies van der Rohe Pavilion in Barcelona), lamps by Jean Perzel and Le Corbusier's chaises longues. The most striking of the 10 unique rooms are the Clément Rousseau Suite (pictured) and Mondrian-inspired Prestige Room. Unusually for the medina, there are indoor and outdoor pools, as well as a spa and hammam.
20 Derb Chtouka, T 0 524 391 926,
www.villamakassar.com

Riad Due
Finding a riad with a contemporary decor is not so hard these days, but the three (Riad Due, Riad 12 and Riad 72) run by Italian photographer-turned-hotelier Giovanna Cinel remain standouts. In the four-room Due, Cinel combines modern furniture with Berber carpets and the work of Marrakechi designers and artists including, in the Zan Suite (above), a hand-beaten copper bath (decorative only) by Yahya Création (see p074). Cinel's design nous can be seen everywhere, from the revamped art deco chairs lining the teal-coloured plunge pool to the ram-horn hooks in the bathrooms. The landscaping is also a highlight – an area of banana palms and ferns in the courtyard contrasts with a cactus garden on the rooftop.
2 Derb Chentouf, T 0 524 387 629, www.uovo.com

Dar Kawa

Buried deep in a knot of streets close to the Ben Youssef complex (see p068) and Musée de Marrakech (T 0 524 441 893), Dar Kawa's hard-to-find address may seem daunting. But for visitors wanting to feel the true pulse of the medina, few locations beat it. Opened in 2011, the riad is a collaboration between Belgian textile designer Valerie Barkowski and architect Quentin Wilbaux, who helped restore the 17th-century Saadian house. In a city infused with colour, the pale slate-coloured *zellige* and dove-grey woodwork in the courtyard (above) are refreshing. Of the four rooms, we plumped for the Olamssi Suite, for its appliqué rug and African furniture. On the roof terrace, escape the afternoon heat on the antique day bed. *55 Souk Hal Fassi, Kaat Ben Nahed, T 0 661 344 333, www.darkawa.net*

La Mamounia
Aided by an army of artisans, French interior designer Jacques Garcia brought modern glamour to this storied hotel following a scrupulous restoration. A few years on, the allure remains as strong. The rooms are lavish yet chic, the spa (pictured) is exquisite and the famous gardens enchanting.
Avenue Bab Jdid, T 0 524 388 600, www.mamounia.com

24 HOURS
SEE THE BEST OF THE CITY IN JUST ONE DAY

Marrakech is a city of moments: catching sight of an age-old bakery or the scents of the spice souk as you meander through the medina are things that will make your visit memorable. The best way to discover the old city is to get out into the fray. Start at the epicentre, Jemaa El Fna. Mornings are the square's down time. After dark, it's a frenzy of merchants, musicians and soothsayers. Le Salama (40 rue des Banques, T 0 524 391 300) is a charming spot for a low-key brunch. The souks (see p072) are the area's main attractions, but they can be a tourist trap. A subtler introduction to local culture is Maison de la Photographie (opposite).

The new town is Marrakech at its most strollable. Explore the city's growing contemporary art scene, starting at David Bloch Gallery (see p078), on one of the *ville*'s most fashionable streets, followed by the photography-focused Galerie 127 (127 avenue Mohammed V, T 0 524 432 667) and Matisse Art Gallery (61 rue de Yougoslavie, T 0 524 448 326). If you have time, drive out to the nascent Musée de la Palmeraie (Dar Tounsi, Route de Fès, T 0 610 408 096), launched in 2011 by Abderrazak Benchabane as a showcase for Moroccan artists. The museum at Jardin Majorelle (see p034) is now dedicated to Berber culture, and is well worth a tour, as is the shop (see p082). Across the road, 33 Rue Majorelle (see p036) gathers together the best of modern Moroccan design. *For full addresses, see Resources.*

10.30 Maison de la Photographie

This peaceful courtyard gallery offers a photographic inroad to Moroccan history. Owners Patrick Manac'h and Hamid Mergani bought the house in the mid medina to house their private collection of vintage photographs. Displayed chronologically over several floors, the exhibition begins downstairs with images of Tangier taken in the late 19th century. Also on view is the first colour film of Berber culture, made by Daniel Chicault in 1957. Linger on the roof terrace for a drink and enjoy the sweeping view over the old city. In the village of Tafza, about 35 minutes' drive from Marrakech, Manac'h and Mergani have set up the Ecomusée Berbère, which focuses on rural life and crafts. *46 rue Ahal Fès, T 0 524 385 721, www.maisondelaphotographie.ma*

12.00 Jardin Majorelle
French artist Jacques Majorelle arrived
in Marrakech in 1919, painting it profusely
in the style of the orientalists, whose
frequently erotic visions of Arab and Asian
societies titillated Western fin-de-siècle
salons. But it is these exuberant gardens,
framed in a cobalt colour called Majorelle
blue, that represent his true legacy.
Wandering along the raised walkways will
take you on a mesmerising journey across
lily ponds and into a world of rare plants
and flowers. The garden was rescued from
disrepair in 1980 by Yves Saint Laurent
and his partner, Pierre Bergé, and the
fashion designer's ashes are scattered
here. After taking in the flora, dip into
the culture and crafts of Morocco's native
Berber tribes, in the renovated museum
housed in Paul Sinoir's 1931 building (right).
Most striking is the jewellery collection.
Avenue Yacoub El Mansour,
T 0 524 301 852, www.jardinmajorelle.com

13.30 33 Rue Majorelle

This pioneering shop sells the work of some 60 designers. Founded by interior designer Yehia Abdelnour, Monique Bresson, buyer for Amanjena's boutique, and restaurateur Norya Nemiche, the venue is three projects in one. Kaowa (opposite) is an eaterie dedicated to healthy 'fast food' and juices; the couscous on Fridays and briouats are not to be missed. The gallery (above), lined with art and furniture, is Abdelnour's domain and doubles as extra café seating. In the rest of the store, browse Bresson's keen edit of products and fashion talent, including Amine Bendriouich (see p062). For the design of the space itself, architects Imaad Rahmouni (Kaowa) and Arnaud Gilles (the boutique) collaborated with the founders.
33 rue Yves Saint Laurent, T 0 524 314 195, www.33ruemajorelle.com

20.00 L'Avenue
This lively corner of Guéliz is where the area's habitués gather at the weekend. L'Avenue avoids the self-consciousness of some of the city's newer venues and its dark, deco-inspired interior is one of the most comfortable dining rooms in town. The modern French and Italian cuisine is beautifully presented too.
Route de Targa/Rue du Capitaine Arigui, T 0 524 458 901

URBAN LIFE
CAFÉS, RESTAURANTS, BARS AND NIGHTCLUBS

Like the distinct personalities of the medina and the new town, Marrakech nightlife will either have you lazing on a candlelit terrace sipping mint tea or dancing with abandon next to a scantily clad local. There's a growing trend for a European-style slickness, but venues don't get bogged down in fashion. Clubs here, such as Djellabar (see p060), are fun and playful in their design. The cool spots are in Guéliz, including Dahab Club at La Rennaissance (see p016), and, more recently, Hivernage, where Marrakechis rub shoulders with out-of-towners at places like Mooï (see p044) and SO Night Lounge (Rue Haroun Errachid, T 0 656 515 009).

The restaurant culture is modernising too, with an influx of international chefs lured by the idea of reworking Moroccan cuisine, which is notoriously heavy. For a traditional meal, the better-known establishments in the medina may excite with their decor and entertainment, but the food and the service can be less impressive and the clientele made up almost exclusively of tourists. One exception is the charming Les Trois Saveurs (see p053). Among the modern eateries, we recommend restaurant and *bar à vin* Le Studio (85 boulevard Moulay Rachid, T 0 524 433 700), L'Avenue (see p038) and Mooï (see p044). For classic dishes, it's worth trying your riad, which will likely have a cook. It may be some of the best food you'll eat, in the loveliest surroundings.
For full addresses, see Resources.

Ziwana

Moroccan artist Med Hajlani's lounge-cum-restaurant is unlike any other venue in Marrakech. Carved out of a riad in the south-west medina, it's an enchanting, fantastical space. Some of the forms and motifs are recognisably Moroccan, others are unique. 'Ziwana is a pure flight of my imagination,' says Hajlani, who spent 10 years designing and realising his vision. There are four salons, including the courtyard area (above), main dining room, music room and *fumoir*, culminating in a spectacular roof terrace. Hajlani also created the wrought-iron furniture, some of which has been displayed at the Jean Nouvel-designed Institut du Monde Arabe in Paris. If you're looking for a venue for a soirée or a private dinner, this is it.
5-6 Derb El Maada, T 0 524 380 800, www.ziwana.com

SkyBAB

One of the sleekest addresses in town, BAB Hotel marked the debut of architect Clémence Pirajean, daughter of its French owners and founder of Studio Hopscotch in London. Reshaping a 1980s apartment block, Pirajean created a contemporary 45-room property, whose blocky balconies and showy swimming pool lend the place a mod Marrakech-meets-Miami vibe. Local touches include Lala Mika's lamps made from recycled plastic bags, and art deco pieces found in the souks. At the bar/lounge, SkyBAB, an in-crowd arrives for cocktails, before heading downstairs to the restaurant, where Michelin-starred chef Alain Le Rest proves his skills, particularly with fish. *Boulevard El Mansour Eddahbi, T 0 524 435 250, www.babhotelmarrakech.com*

Mooï

After several years spent exploring Morocco and its coastline, Fabien Pauleau hung up his scuba gear to join his family in building Mooï – a boutique hotel, club and restaurant. The architecture and decor are both his vision. His aim was to create a venue that was minimal without being stiff, appealing to young locals as much as to tourists. It took four years to complete, opening in 2011, and is ideally placed at the heart of the new town's nightlife. The white interior relies on clever lighting for ambience and includes a smattering of pop art. You could spend an evening here. Start with drinks on the terrace, move to the restaurant, Fresh, for Mediterranean-inspired food, then slip down to the club (left). At weekends, there are live bands or sets from Morocco's first female DJ, Djette Katy M, or the likes of David Vendetta. *Avenue Echouhada, T 0 524 434 306, www.le-mooi.com*

Le Jardin

Local mover and shaker Kamal Laftimi opened this eaterie, housed in a 17th-century riad, in 2011. He conceived the design with Anne Favier, who wanted to create an urban oasis, echoing the trees already growing in the courtyard. Divided into various sections, the venue encompasses a library/living room (above) and dining area (opposite). Upstairs, there's a shop selling books, and items by local designers. Le Jardin has become a popular medina hangout, as has Laftimi's other enterprise, Terrasse des Épices (see p050). Stop by for lunch while you're shopping in the souks, or for some tea and cake. Unusually for the medina (and testament to Laftimi's negotiating skills), Le Jardin has a licence to sell alcohol.
32 Souk El Jeld, Sidi Abdelaziz,
T 0 524 378 295, www.lejardin.ma

Le Zinc
Several eateries have opened in Sidi
Ghanem over the past few years, with
varying success. Le Zinc has been a hit,
thanks to French chef Damien Durand.
His bistro wouldn't look out of place
in the 2e arrondissement of Paris. Drop
by for lunch and a plate of staunchly
French fare, and wines by the glass.
*517 avenue Principale, ZI Sidi Ghanem,
T 0 524 335 969*

Terrasse des Épices

A stylish pitstop during a sweep through the souks below, this rooftop eaterie injects a certain Sahara chic into the medina. It's co-owned by Kamal Laftimi and Nicolas Nancy, who also launched Café des Épices (T 0 524 391 770) on Place Rahba Lakdima. The design is a collaboration with Anne Favier and marries dark *tadelakt* with shots of colour in the furniture and the textiles.

Retreat to one of the cabanas and cool off with a fresh juice. The menu is ideal lunch fare — mostly salads, and grilled meat and fish. In the evening, Terrasse des Épices is a neighbourhood meeting point for a fashionable group of locals and a chilled-out spot for a sundowner and a light supper.
15 Souk Cherifia, Sidi Abdelaziz, T 0 524 375 904, www.terrassedesepices.com

La Cuisine de Mona

This bijou Lebanese eaterie moved across the street from its previous location in late 2010. Few taxi drivers seem able to find it (ask for the Victor Hugo school and they'll get you there), but it's worth the hunt. Tucked down a residential street, the tiny terrace will pop out at you with its hot-pink and apple-green colours. Despite its diminutive size, the restaurant is extremely popular for lunch and dinner; to date, it's still a mostly Moroccan haunt. Order owner/chef Mona Farah's lemonade, made with a dash of orange blossom water, and mezze platter, comprising dishes such as tabbouleh and smoky baba ganoush. The flatbread stuffed with spiced lamb, and *mouhalabiyeh* (yogurt with pistachio nuts and orange blossom water) are divine. *Résidence Mamoune 5, 115b, Quartier El Ghoul cite OLM, T 0 618 137 959*

Les Trois Saveurs at La Maison Arabe

La Maison Arabe's roots go back to 1946, when Frenchwoman Hélène Sébillon-Larochette and her daughter, Suzy, were granted permission by the then pasha of Marrakech to open a restaurant in the old city. It was the first of its kind and soon attracted a high-profile clientele, including Churchill. In 1995, the venue was bought by another innovator, current owner Fabrizio Ruspoli, who renovated and extended it to create the first boutique hotel in the medina. Today, La Maison Arabe has two restaurants, including Les Trois Saveurs, which presents a distinct take on local cuisine. Dine in the salon (above) or on the terrace (overleaf). Either way, don't miss it: this is one of the most romantic eateries in town, with a unique atmosphere.
1 Derb Assehbe, T 0 524 387 010, www.lamaisonarabe.com

Les Trois Saveurs at La Maison Arabe

Le Grand Café de la Poste

Dating from 1925, this building is one of the oldest in Guéliz. Back then, it was known as the Grand Hotel and served travellers making their way to the Red City. It was reborn in 2005 as Le Grand Café de la Poste (taking its name from the huge post office across the road). Downstairs, the colonial vibe has been retained, with rattan chairs, potted palms and whirring ceiling fans. The mezzanine lounge was fashioned after one of the bars at La Mamounia (see p030) in the 1920s. Le Salon (above) on the first floor attracts new-town urbanites for cocktails in the evening. For seasoned regulars, of which there are many, the best spot is the terrace, with a kir or glass of fizz and a dozen Marennes-Oléron oysters. *Place du 16 Novembre, T 0 524 433 038, www.grandcafedelaposte.com*

Dar Cherifa

Close to Jemaa El Fna, this splendid 'literary café' and art gallery is set in an early 15th-century riad, where the original details have been stripped back and allowed to breathe. The owner, Abdellatif Ben Abdellah, is a local cultural doyen and renovator of numerous riads in the medina. Here, he organises readings, exhibitions and music events. Arrive for a light lunch (order some salads – candied tomatoes, slices of courgette marinated in olive oil and lemon juice, and peppery aubergine, to name a few), or some mint tea and pastries. Spend time admiring the architecture and scanning Dar Cherifa's selection of books on Moroccan art and crafts. Quiz your waiter or waitress for the date of the next soirée.

8 Derb Chorfa Lakhir, T 0 524 426 463, www.marrakech-riads.net

Azar
This is a project by Moroccan designer
Younes Duret, who was hired by Marcel
and Grégory Chiche, owners of local
institution Le Comptoir Darna (T 0 524
437 702). The neo-orientalist Azar
launched in 2010 and is still hip. Feast
on the Lebanese food in the restaurant
(pictured), then dance it off downstairs.
*Rue de Yougoslavie, T 0 524 430 920,
www.azar-marrakech.com*

Djellabar
Claude Challe (the creative force behind
Buddha Bar) made his Red City debut
with the cheeky restaurant/club Djellabar.
The space was originally a wedding room,
and the fabulous original features (*zellige*
and elaborate stucco) have been kept.
Along with co-owner Stéphane Atlas,
Challe can often be spotted holding court.
Villa Bougainvillée, 2 rue Abou Hanifa,
T 0 524 421 242, www.djellabar.com

INSIDER'S GUIDE

AMINE BENDRIOUICH, FASHION DESIGNER

Marrakech-born Amine Bendriouich is a rising talent on the Moroccan design scene. A frequent commuter between Berlin and Casablanca, where his label Couture & Bullshit (www.ab-cb.com) is based, he's always seduced when he returns home. 'The colours, the people, the surroundings, where you can ski, swim or just chill, are magical,' he says. He suggests visitors stay at Fellah Hotel (see p017), checking out its Dar Al-Ma'mûn arts centre, or artist Hassan Hajjaj's Riad Yima (32 Derb Aajane, Rahba Lakdima, T 0 524 391 987), for a sample of contemporary Marrakechi culture.

His collection is on sale at 33 Rue Majorelle (see p036), so he often grabs breakfast at Kaowa. For an upmarket lunch, he likes to sit poolside at Dar Moha (81 rue Dar El Bacha, T 0 524 386 400). A street stall called Tihane near the Saadian Tombs (see p065) is 'great for a late-night sandwich'. 'A decent live music scene is still lacking in Marrakech,' he concedes, which is why he's working on a music programme for Dam Arts (www.dam-arts.org) in 2012. 'Hopefully, the collaboration will give birth to a venue where people can have a real party and a new experience,' he says. When he's not busy planning Marrakech's next cultural revolution, you'll find him kicking back at Flower Power Café at Casa Botanica (Route de Sidi Abdellah Ghiat, T 0 524 484 087) or rebooting at La Sultana Spa (403 rue de la Kasbah, T 0 524 388 008).

For full addresses, see Resources.

ARCHITOUR
A GUIDE TO MARRAKECH'S ICONIC BUILDINGS

Historic Arab construction is, by nature, inward-looking and private. Add the fact that most mosques are closed to non-Muslims and you'll see why much of the city's architectonic eye candy is to be found in the detail. In one sense, the hotel-riad phenomenon has been a saving grace. Many of these houses were wrecks before the boom. Not only did their renovation rekindle the dying local arts of stucco, mosaic and woodwork, it made much of the city's architecture accessible for the price of a room or a meal. From the 1970s onwards, the New Moroccan style, developed by architects such as Stuart Church and Charles Boccara, and designer Bill Willis, transformed several ruins into stunning palaces. More recently, Jacques Garcia spent three years working with master artisans (maâlems) to restore the faded features of La Mamounia (see p030).

The new town deserves an architectural renaissance. While developments such as Christian de Portzamparc's CasArt complex in Casablanca and Zaha Hadid's Rabat Grand Theatre forge ahead, Marrakech lags behind in terms of similarly ambitious projects. However, plans are afoot for a 4,000 sq m Islamic arts museum by architect Moulay Assaid Lalaoui, and a new training centre for sustainable construction, whose design won a 2011 Holcim Award. Meanwhile, there's plenty to savour in the city's monuments, which tell a dogged history of occupation and exceptional craftsmanship. *For full addresses, see Resources.*

Saadian Tombs

Marrakech's Saadian period (the dynasty ruled Morocco from 1554-1669) has been dubbed its golden age – literally. The Saads had a voracious appetite for gold, and used it in abundance in their palaces and garden pavilions. But if they knew how to live, they knew how to die as well. The Saadian Tombs in the Kasbah district are so exquisite that even the dynasty's conquerors, the Alaouites, chose to leave them intact when ransacking the city. The 66 tombs are distributed over two buildings, with separate rooms for the kings, their wives and children, and a more sombre chamber for servants. The centrepiece is the Hall of Twelve Columns (above), where the tombs' creator, Sultan Ahmed El Mansour, lies beneath a marble tombstone set on a glorious *zellige* floor. *Rue de la Kasbah*

Palais El Badi

This opulent complex was commissioned in 1578 by Ahmed El Mansour, who hired craftsmen from all over the country and imported about 50 tons of marble for the job. The palace's incredible internal riches were legendary, until they were pillaged by Alaouite leader Moulay Ismaïl, to help him complete his own palace in Meknes. Rambling ruins are all that remain.

Place des Ferblantiers

Koubba El Badiyin

Part of the Ben Youssef complex, which also includes a mosque (not accessible by non-Muslims) and Koranic school, or *medersa* (overleaf), is this *koubba*, an ornamental dome that usually contains the remains of a holy man. *Koubbas* are normally off-limits to visitors, but this one is an exception. Dating from the 12th century, it's the only intact relic of the Almoravids' reign in the city, and is most appealing once you get beyond the excavated rubble and the ablution basins. The interior of the dome is embellished with delicate floral and star motifs, surrounded by keyhole arches.
Off Rue Souk El Khemis, T 0 524 441 893

Ben Youssef Medersa

Nowhere in Marrakech is the influence of the Andalusian style as evident as in this *medersa*. Dating from the 14th century, it was rebuilt by the Saadians in 1565, when Marrakech's *medersas* were considered great centres of learning and the gold-rich sultans were throwing their lavish assets into the rundown city. This was a functioning school until 1960 and was opened to the public in 1982. After passing through the long entrance hall, you come to the building's focal point (right) – the grand courtyard and pool, where the students would have carried out their ritualistic ablutions. This is enclosed by arabesque stucco arches, *zellige* and carved cedarwood friezes. It's worth ascending to the dorms on the upper floors. According to the tour guides, 900 boys once cooked, ate and slept in these tiny spartan cells.
Off Rue Souk El Khemis

SHOPPING

THE BEST RETAIL THERAPY AND WHAT TO BUY

Everyone will tell you that the best craftsmen come from Fez, but aficionados agree that the best shopping is in Marrakech. Lately, a new wave of Moroccan designers has come to the fore, which you should check out at 33 Rue Majorelle (see p036) and at Galerie du Souk Cherifia (Souk Cherifia, Sidi Abdelaziz) in the medina.

Most traditional crafts are executed in the tiny workshops north of Jemaa El Fna and the specialist souks off Souk Smarine and Rue Mouassine. Haggling is expected, and for this you'll need sharp bargaining powers; prepare to pay between a half and two-thirds of the starting price. Not everything will translate well back home, though. For modish Beni Ouarain carpets, try Lahandira (Foundouk Namouss, 100 Derb Sidi Ishak, T 0 665 357 911); Chez les Frères Kassri (3 Souk Dylaouine, T 0 662 405 102) sells plain blankets; and La Maison Bahira (Boutique 52, 15 Souk Cherifia, T 0 524 386 365) stocks fine table linens. The one-stop shop for oriental items is Mustapha Blaoui (142-144 Bab Doukkala, T 0 524 385 240).

The modern shops are in Guéliz, particularly on Rue de la Liberté and Rue des Vieux Marrakchis. As a design destination, the new town is eclipsing the industrial zone Sidi Ghanem, which is a 15-minute taxi ride away. The area is still worth a visit, though, notably Atelier Nihal (see p076), Fenyadi (see p084) and Florence Teillet (T 0 661 225 905; appointment only) for handwoven textiles. *For full addresses, see Resources.*

Popham Design

Caitlin and Samuel Dowe-Sandes founded Popham Design in 2006, when they relocated from the US to Marrakech and began renovating a riad. Unable to find tiles that suited their modern taste, they decided to design a range themselves. Several years on, their business is thriving. Handmade from cement, the tiles are crafted by a team of local artisans in Popham's small factory just outside the city, using production methods that make as little impact on the environment as possible. Many of the patterns, such as 'Diamond-in-the-Rough' (above; 1,500 dirhams per sq m), allow for the tiles to be laid out in various configurations. All the products are suitable for interior and exterior use.
*Route de l'Ourika km7, Tasseltante,
T 0 666 011 646, www.pophamdesign.com*

Yahya Création

Arguably the city's most prolific, and secretive, designer, Yahya Rouach crafts intricate lanterns, lights and bespoke items in copper, brass and silver, using a filigree method that can appear as fine as needlework. It was during a trip to Marrakech in 2004 that Rouach became fascinated by the beaten metalwork he witnessed in the souks, and began noting down ideas that combined the craft with contemporary lines and shapes. He moved to Marrakech a year later. Today he employs some 200 craftsmen to supply a client list that includes royals, Hollywood A-listers and Marrakech's luxury hotels. A recent project, shown at L'Institut du Monde Arabe in Paris, is a collaboration with calligrapher Mehdi Qotbi that explores the art of writing and sculpture.
49-50 passage Ghandouri,
61 rue de Yougoslavie, T 0 524 422 776,
www.yahyacreation.com

Atelier Nihal

Marion Verdier worked as a stylist for the French fashion press before setting up her own atelier in Marrakech in 2003. Currently, she hires between 12 and 16 artisans, who work with hand-cut patterns on traditional looms to create her sought-after textiles. Verdier's signature technique is to incorporate metallic threads, strips of butter-soft leather, sequins and delicate beads into a fine wool and cotton weave. The materials, which all have a subtle shimmer, are then used to make bedspreads, cushions, wall hangings and curtains. Her textiles appear in many of the city's chicest riads and she also designs furniture, for which she accepts bespoke commissions. If you're looking for a carry-on gift, ask to see her totes. Visits are by appointment only.
266 ZI Sidi Ghanem, T 0 671 160 162

Kaftan Queen

Sarah Rouach's boutique on an up-and-coming shopping strip in Guéliz is a boon for women in search of modern Moroccan fashion. Using new and vintage fabrics, and different styles of embroidery (one of the specialist crafts of Morocco), Rouach produces mostly kaftans and draped dresses. The designs meld oriental and Western forms, resulting in pieces that are elegant and modern. In 2011, she expanded the range to include embellished *babouches* (the leather slippers you'll see all over the medina), belts with intricate buckles designed by her husband, Yahya Rouach (see p074), silver clutches, and leather bags with a metallic trim.
10 Immeuble Jaccard, Avenue Mohammed Bequal/Avenue Mohammed V,
www.kaftanqueenmorocco.com

David Bloch Gallery
Local art galleries are launching thick
and fast. Among the best is David Bloch,
which represents European, American and
Moroccan artists in a warehouse space.
The gallery promotes contemporary work,
particularly the street art movement and
Marrakechis like Larbi Cherkaoui ('Hall
of Fame IV' group show, 2011, pictured).
*8 bis, Rue des Vieux Marrakchis, T 0 524
457 595, www.davidblochgallery.com*

Lalla Studio

Former personal shopper Laetitia Trouillet opened Lalla Studio as a place to design her own goods, display her cache of vintage Moroccan finds, and consult on sourcing items in the medina. The minimal, light-filled space has quickly become a meeting point for buyers, journalists and fashionistas looking for unusual items. Trouillet's own designs include cultish handbags, such as the 1980s 'Tourista' tote and kitschy camel-motif carpetbags, scarves and chunky jewellery. From 2012, she plans to invite guest designers, international and local, to showcase their work, from textiles to furniture, in the studio. Trouillet also sells her products at Galerie du Souk Cherifia (see p072) and 33 Rue Majorelle (see p036), as well as at Paul & Joe, among other boutiques, in London, Paris and Switzerland.
5 rue de la Liberté, T 0 661 477 228, www.lalla.fr

Majorelle Boutique

The original boutique at Jardin Majorelle (see p034) opened in 2001, in a space designed by the late Bill Willis. The shop was the brainchild of Pierre Bergé, who wanted to promote the diverse range of crafts produced in Morocco and objects inspired by the work of Yves Saint Laurent. Fellow fashion luminary Bernard Sanz took over direction of the store in 2005, and presided over its relaunch in 2010.

Sanz first visited Marrakech in 1966, and has harboured a fascination for Morocco's artisanship ever since. The crafts section (opposite) sells items spanning Tamgrout terracotta to textiles and Sanz's own jewellery. The bookshop (above) is part art gallery, curated by ex-Christie's auctioneer Patrick Martin.
Avenue Yacoub El Mansour, T 0 524 301 852, www.jardinmajorelle.com

Fenyadi

When three of Sidi Ghanem's prime design businesses – Akkal (ceramics by Charlotte Barkowski), Via Notti (textiles) and Amira Bougies (ornamental candles) – sold their individual concerns in 2010, they decided to come together under one roof and one brand. Fenyadi is spread over three floors of a converted warehouse, giving each product type plenty of display room. The original designers create a new range each season, coordinating with one another to produce a unified interior-design collection. For autumn 2011, the common theme was the landscape of the Sahara, which inspired a palette of sand, burnt umber, yellow ochre, blue and green. A flagship Fenyadi store is due to open in Casablanca in 2012. *219 ZI Sidi Ghanem, T 0 524 356 024, www.fenyadi.com*

Ministero del Gusto

When Alessandra Lippini, former fashion editor of Italian *Vogue*, and furniture designer Fabrizio Bizzarri opened 'the ministry of taste' in 1998, shockwaves rippled through the souks. Rather than restoring the space they moved into, they created one. Part showroom, part gallery, it echoes the sand houses of Mali and has fireplaces that recall the ceremonial

jewellery of Ghana. The collection of items is equally interesting and eclectic. You might come across antique Murano glass chandeliers, original 'Elda' chairs by Joe Colombo, and, upstairs, a selection of vintage haute couture; past gems have included a Chanel dress once owned by Liza Minnelli. *22 Derb Azzouz, T 0 524 426 455, www.ministerodelgusto.com*

SPORTS AND SPAS
WORK OUT, CHILL OUT OR JUST WATCH

At first, this may not seem like a city that will stretch your muscles beyond lugging your shopping back to your hotel, but it has lots to offer beyond lazy pool days. Top-quality golf clubs have existed here since the city was colonised; two of the most highly regarded are Royal Golf (Route de Ouarzazate, T 0 524 409 828) and L'Amelkis (Route de Ouarzazate km12, T 0 524 404 414). One of the more unusual places to play a round, or go horse riding, is the eerily atmospheric desert resort of La Pause, in the Agafay hills (Douar Lmih Laroussiène, Commune Agafay, T 0 661 306 494), where you can stay overnight. The Atlas Mountains have a sprinkling of pistes, and the resort of Oukaïmeden, about 80km south of the city, is due to receive a major overhaul by the Dubai-based company Emaar.

As with the hotels, spas in Marrakech aim for ever new heights of luxury. Among the best are Angsana (57-58 rue de la Bahia, T 0 524 380 978), Royal Mansour (opposite) and La Mamounia (see p030). You'll find most Marrakechis at their local hammam. The medina has one in every quarter, and it's wise to have an idea of the etiquette before you go in: buy a tub of *savon noir* and a glove at the entrance, leave your lower undies on, douse yourself in hot and cold water, lather up with soap, then scrub it off. You can hire a staff member to do the *gommage* (scrub). Our preferred hammam is the Carlota Spa (see p094) in Guéliz.

For full addresses, see Resources.

Royal Mansour Spa

This outstanding spa was designed by architects OBMI and covers 2,500 sq m. The white, honeycomb-like structure (overleaf) through which you enter is opulent without being overbearing, and instils an instant sense of calm. The pampering options include a three-room hammam, luxurious treatments using Dr Hauschka, Maroc Maroc or Sisley products, and a Chanel Espace Beauté cabin offering six types of facial. For couples, there are private spa suites. The surrounding gardens, which are dotted with lemon trees, were designed by Madrid-based Luis Vallejo, who drew inspiration from the Alhambra in Granada. Admire them while you lounge by the pool (above), which is bathed in natural light. *Rue Abou Abbas El Sebti, T 0 529 808 200, www.royalmansour.com*

Royal Mansour Spa

Harem

Founded by Sandra Zwollo in 2010, Harem is a women-only retreat held on the private estate of French artist Jean-François Fourtou. The grounds feature several of his artworks, including an intriguing tilted house (opposite). But if you're thinking wheatgrass shots and navel-gazing, think again. Zwollo takes a relaxed approach, offering yoga and meditation classes, beauty treatments, nutritional advice, wine tastings and meals prepared by a chef who adapts Moroccan recipes using Chinese food therapy principles (all inclusive in the full-board fee). Bookings are taken for between six and 14 guests. Eighty per cent of profits go to Fondation Fourtou, which provides education and training for local women and children.
Dar El Sadaka, T +1 347 292 9735/
0 672 091 886, www.harem-escape.com

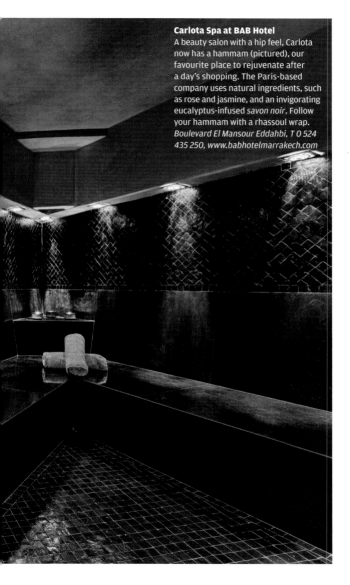

Carlota Spa at BAB Hotel
A beauty salon with a hip feel, Carlota now has a hammam (pictured), our favourite place to rejuvenate after a day's shopping. The Paris-based company uses natural ingredients, such as rose and jasmine, and an invigorating eucalyptus-infused *savon noir*. Follow your hammam with a rhassoul wrap.
Boulevard El Mansour Eddahbi, T 0 524 435 250, www.babhotelmarrakech.com

ESCAPES

WHERE TO GO IF YOU WANT TO LEAVE TOWN

The happy location of Marrakech, cradled between the mountains and the sea, provides plenty of options for skipping town. Less than an hour away, in the foothills of the Atlas, is the Ourika Valley, which can be easily visited in a day for some hiking. If you want to stay longer, the area has numerous hotels, from modest *douars* (traditional Berber houses) to lavish resorts. Kasbah du Toubkal (Imlil, T 0 524 485 611) and Kasbah Bab Ourika (see p102) are both recommended. Alternatively, venture further south-east into the desert. The voguish Erg Chigaga Luxury Camp (El Gouera) is about a nine-hour drive from Marrakech via Ouarzazate (see p100).

Essaouira (see p098) on the Atlantic coast is a revitalising destination after the heat and dust of the Red City. You could make the return journey in a day, but that wouldn't give you much time to explore the city's quirky charms. On Morocco's northern tip, the cosmopolitan Tangier is currently undergoing a renaissance. Villas of Morocco (T 0 522 942 525) has chic private rentals here, or stay at Hôtel Nord-Pinus (11 rue du Riad Sultan, T 0 661 228 140). Fez (opposite) boasts one of the oldest medinas in the Arab world – less manic and even more captivating than the medina in Marrakech. A day trip from Fez, the Roman settlement of Volubilis is less well known than Pompeii but no less splendid, and now has a museum and visitor centre, designed by Tarik Oualalou of Kilo Architectures. *For full addresses, see Resources.*

Fez

A scenic, seven-hour train ride from Marrakech, Fez has some of the most important buildings in the Islamic world, including the vast 9th-century Karaouine Mosque and University, and the shrine of Moulay Idriss II, son of the city's founder. Enter the medina at the striking Bab Boujloud and step back in time. There are no cars and few mopeds, just a riveting stream of people. One area to seek out is the honey souk, which sells rare varieties. Stay at the stunning Dar Seffarine (above; T 0 671 113 528) or Dar Finn (T 0 655 018 975), a hip spin on a riad renovation. Try a camel burger at Café Clock (T 0 535 637 855) or some delicious Fassi food at Fès et Gestes (T 0 535 638 532), located in a peaceful garden. Fez Café (T 0 664 647 679), at Le Jardin des Biehn hotel, also boasts delightful surroundings.

Essaouira

Around two hours' drive west through the desert, whitewashed Essaouira is the antithesis of Marrakech – laidback and devoid of *le jet*-type decadence (for now). The Portuguese first built a fortress here in the early 16th century, though the present city dates to two centuries later. French engineer and architect Théodore Cornut was ordered by the ruling Alaouite sultan to come up with a modern, grid-like layout. Orson Welles shot scenes for his 1952 film version of *Othello* here, and the city has hosted many artists and musicians over the years; Bob Marley and Jimi Hendrix loved the place. The renowned Gnaoua music festival (www.festival-gnaoua.net) is held here each year in June. Although not on the level of Marrakech, the riad scene continues to take shape. The stylish four-room villa Dar Beida (opposite; T 0 667 965 386) combines white-walled cool with Moroccan and retro furnishings.

Ouarzazate
Head 200km south-east of Marrakech and you reach Ouarzazate, threshold of the desert of southern Morocco and Route of the Thousand Kasbahs, which passes through the Drâa, Dades, Todra and Ziz valleys. Many of the fortresses have been turned into hotels. One of the best is Dar Ahlam (T 0 524 852 239), which has nine suites and three villas set in the serene Skoura palm grove.

Kasbah Bab Ourika

Nestled in the Ourika Valley, this 15-room hotel is the creation of owner Stephen Skinner. Joining forces with architect Argus Gathorne-Hardy, he constructed it using the typical Berber building method of *pisé* (rammed earth). For the furnishings, Skinner called in interior designer Romain Michel-Ménière, another devotee of the Berber style; locally sourced textiles and artefacts appear throughout the property. The snug Room 6 (above), a suite, has a fireplace and a private terrace; Room 12 boasts a sunken bath overlooking a red-rock canyon. Day-long treks into the valley will take you to saffron farms and the spectacular Setti Fatma waterfalls. Or simply soak up the scenery from the terrace (opposite) while enjoying some of Bab Ourika's excellent Berber cuisine. *Route d'Ourika, T 0 661 634 234, www.kasbahbabourika.com*

NOTES

SKETCHES AND MEMOS

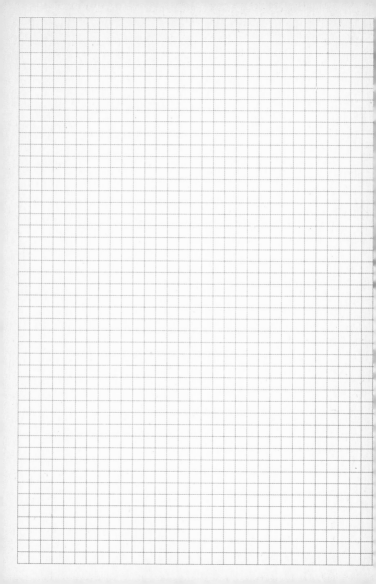

RESOURCES

CITY GUIDE DIRECTORY

A

L'Amelkis Golf Club 088
  Route de Ouarzazate km12
  T 0 524 404 414

Angsana Spa 088
  57-58 rue de la Bahia
  Riad Zitoun Jdid
  T 0 524 380 978
  www.angsanaspa.com

Atelier Nihal 076
  266 ZI Sidi Ghanem
  T 0 671 160 162

L'Avenue 038
  Route de Targa/Rue du Capitaine Arigui
  T 0 524 458 901

Azar 058
  Rue de Yougoslavie
  T 0 524 430 920
  www.azar-marrakech.com

B

Ben Youssef Medersa 070
  Off Rue Souk El Khemis

C

Café Clock 097
  7 Derb El Magana
  Fez
  T 0 535 637 855
  www.cafeclock.com

Café des Épices 050
  75 place Rahba Lakdima
  T 0 524 391 770
  www.cafedesepices.net

Carlota Spa 094
  BAB Hotel
  Boulevard El Mansour Eddahbi
  T 0 524 435 250
  www.babhotelmarrakech.com

Chez les Frères Kassri 072
  3 Souk Dylaouine
  T 0 662 405 102

Le Comptoir Darna 059
  Avenue Echouhada
  T 0 524 437 702
  www.comptoirdarna.com

La Cuisine de Mona 052
  Résidence Mamoune 5
  115b
  Quartier El Ghoul cite OLM
  T 0 618 137 959

D

Dar Al-Ma'mûn 017
  Fellah Hotel
  Route de l'Ourika km13
  T 0 525 065 000
  www.dam-arts.org

Dar Cherifa 057
  8 Derb Chorfa Lakhir
  T 0 524 426 463
  www.marrakech-riads.net

Dar Moha 062
  81 rue Dar El Bacha
  T 0 524 386 400
  www.darmoha.ma

David Bloch Gallery 078
  8 bis, Rue des Vieux Marrakchis
  T 0 524 457 595
  www.davidblochgallery.com

Djellabar 060
  Villa Bougainvillée
  2 rue Abou Hanifa
  T 0 524 421 242
  www.djellabar.com

HOTELS
ADDRESSES AND ROOM RATES

César Hôtel 016
Room rates:
double, from 1,700 dirhams
Route de l'Ourika
T 0 524 369 900
www.hotel-cesar-marrakech.com

Dar Ahlam 100
Room rates:
double, from 5,450 dirhams;
Villa, from 9,000 dirhams
Palmeraie de Skoura
Province de Ouarzazate
T 0 524 852 239
www.darahlam.com

Dar Beida 098
Room rates:
double, from 4,000 dirhams per
person per week
141 rue Ibn Khaldoun
Essaouira
T 0 667 965 386
www.castlesinthesand.com

Dar Finn 097
Room rates:
double, from 750 dirhams
27 Zqaq Rowah
Chrablyine
Fez
T 0 655 018 975
www.darfinn.com

Dar Kawa 029
Room rates:
double, from 2,800 dirhams;
Olmassi Suite, 17,000 dirhams
55 Souk Hal Fassi
Kaat Ben Nahed
T 0 661 344 333
www.darkawa.net

Dar Sabra 024
Room rates:
double, from 1,650 dirhams;
Solorzano Suite, 2,130 dirhams
Douar Abbiad
T 0 524 329 172
www.darsabra.com

Dar Seffarine 097
Room rates:
double, from 770 dirhams
14 Derb Sbaa Louyate
Fez
T 0 671 113 528
www.darseffarine.com

Erg Chigaga Luxury Camp 096
Room rates:
tent, 2,785 dirhams per person
per night (minimum 2 nights)
El Gouera
www.desertcampmorocco.com

Fellah Hotel 017
Room rates:
double, 1,460 dirhams;
Suite 103, 4,400 dirhams
Route de l'Ourika km13
T 0 525 065 000
www.fellah-hotel.com

Four Seasons 016
Room rates:
double, 3,700 dirhams
1 avenue de la Ménara
T 0 524 359 200
www.fourseasons.com/marrakech

Habibi Homes 016
Rates: prices on request
T 011 409 984
www.habibihomes.com

Kasbah Bab Ourika 102
Room rates:
double, from 1,650 dirhams;
Room 6, from 3,135 dirhams;
Room 12, from 3,135 dirhams
Route de l'Ourika
Ourika
T 0 661 634 234
www.kasbahbabourika.com

Kasbah du Toubkal 096
Room rates:
double, 1,430 dirhams
Imlil
T 0 524 485 611
www.kasbahdutoubkal.com

La Mamounia 030
Room rates:
double, from 6,000 dirhams
Avenue Bab Jdid
T 0 524 388 600
www.mamounia.com

Mooï 016
Room rates:
double, from 1,200 dirhams;
Avenue Echouhada
T 0 524 434 306
www.le-mooi.com

Hôtel Nord-Pinus 096
Room rates:
double, from 2,240 dirhams
11 rue du Riad Sultan
Tangier
T 0 661 228 140
www.nord-pinus-tanger.com

La Pause 088
Room rates:
double, from 1,680 dirhams
Douar Lmih Laroussiène
Commune Agafay
T 0 661 306 494
www.lapause-marrakech.com

Pearl 016
Room rates:
double, 4,000 dirhams
Avenue Echouhada
T 0 524 424 100
www.hivernage-collection.com

La Renaissance 016
Room rates:
double, from 1,100 dirhams
89 boulevard Zerktouni
T 0 524 337 777
www.renaissance-hotel-marrakech.com

Riad 12 028
Room rates:
double, from 1,780 dirhams
12 Derb Sraghnas
Dar El Bacha
T 0 524 387 629
www.uovo.com

Riad 72 028
Room rates:
double, from 1,390 dirhams
72 Arset Aouzal
T 0 524 387 629
www.uovo.com

Riad Due 028
Room rates:
double, from 1,590 dirhams;
Zan Suite, from 2,130 dirhams
2 Derb Chentouf
T 0 524 387 629
www.uovo.com

Riad Joya 021
  Room rates:
  double, 1,800 dirhams;
  Dar Arabe Suite, 3,000 dirhams
  Hay Moussaine
  Derb al Hammam 26-27
  T 0 524 391 624
  www.riadjoya.com

Riad Tarabel 020
  Room rates:
  double, from 1,930 dirhams;
  Palmeraie Suite, from 4,200 dirhams
  8 Derb Sraghna
  Dar El Bacha
  T 0 524 391 706
  www.riadtarabel.com

Royal Mansour 022
  Room rates:
  One-bedroom riad, from 16,820 dirhams
  Rue Abou Abbas El Sebti
  T 0 529 808 080
  www.royalmansour.com

Villa Makassar 026
  Room rates:
  double, from 1,760 dirhams;
  Prestige Room, 1,900 dirhams;
  Clément Rousseau Suite, 6,120 dirhams
  20 Derb Chtouka
  T 0 524 391 926
  www.villamakassar.com

Villas of Morroco 096
  Room rates:
  Villas, from 1,650 dirhams
  Tangier
  T 0 522 942 525
  www.villasofmorocco.com

WALLPAPER* CITY GUIDES

Executive Editor
Rachael Moloney

Authors
Tara Stevens
Suzanne Wales

Art Director
Loran Stosskopf
Art Editor
Eriko Shimazaki
Designer
Mayumi Hashimoto
Map Illustrator
Russell Bell

Photography Editor
Sophie Corben
Acting Photography Editor
Anika Burgess
Photography Assistant
Nabil Butt

Chief Sub-Editor
Nick Mee

Editorial Assistant
Emma Harrison

Interns
Kate Cregan
Nicola Ferlei-Brown
Mónica R Goya
Nicole Micha

**Wallpaper* Group
Editor-in-Chief**
Tony Chambers
Publishing Director
Gord Ray
Managing Editor
Jessica Diamond
Acting Managing Editor
Oliver Adamson

Wallpaper* ® is a
registered trademark
of IPC Media Limited

First published 2007
Second edition (revised
and updated) 2010
Third edition (revised and
updated) 2012

All prices are correct at
the time of going to press,
but are subject to change.

Printed in China

PHAIDON

Phaidon Press Limited
Regent's Wharf
All Saints Street
London N1 9PA

Phaidon Press Inc
180 Varick Street
New York, NY 10014

Phaidon® is a registered
trademark of Phaidon
Press Limited

www.phaidon.com

A CIP Catalogue record for
this book is available from
the British Library.

ISBN 978 0 7148 64365

PHOTOGRAPHERS

Milo Keller
Koutoubia Mosque,
pp010-011
Ramparts, pp012-013
Dar Cherifa, p057
Saadian Tombs, p065
Palais El Badi, pp066-067
Koubba El Badiyin,
p068, p069
Ben Youssef
Medersa, pp070-071

Nagib Khazaka
Menara Gardens,
pp014-015
Fellah Hotel,
p017, pp018-019
Riad Joya, p021
Royal Mansour, pp022-023
Villa Makassar, pp026-027
Dar Kawa, p029
33 Rue Majorelle,
p036, p037
L'Avenue, pp038-039
Mooï, pp044-045
Le Jardin, p046, p047
Le Zinc, pp048-049
La Cuisine de Mona, p052
Les Trois Saveurs at
La Maison Arabe,
p053, pp054-055
Djellabar, pp060-061

Amine Bendriouich, p063
Yahya Création, pp074-075
Kaftan Queen, p077
David Bloch Gallery,
pp078-079
Lalla Studio, pp080-081
Majorelle Boutique,
p082, p083
Fenyadi, pp084-085
Royal Mansour Spa,
p089, pp090-091
Harem, p092, p093
Carlota Spa at
BAB Hotel, pp094-095

Moroccan Tourist Office
Essaouira, p098
Ouarzazate, pp100-101

Peartree Digital
'Diamond-in-the-Rough'
tiles, p073

James Reeve
Riad Tarabel, p020
Dar Sabra, p024, p025
Riad Due, p028
Maison de la
Photographie, p033
Ziwana, p041
SkyBAB, pp042-043
Terrasse des
Épices, pp050-051
Le Grand Café de
la Poste, p056

Azar, pp058-059
Atelier Nihal, p076
Ministero del
Gusto, pp086-087

Jean-Michel Ruiz
Marrakech city view,
inside front cover

MARRAKECH
A COLOUR-CODED GUIDE TO THE HOT 'HOODS

SOUTH MEDINA
Overrun with mopeds and tourists, but unmissable for a taste of the old city

PALMERAIE
Luxury resorts and spas are hidden amid the palm trees of this tranquil desert oasis

NORTH MEDINA
Beyond the fascinating souks and Ben Youssef complex, explore a quieter Marrakech

HIVERNAGE
This tree-lined quarter is fast developing a sophisticated hotel and nightlife scene

MELLAH/KASBAH
The most interesting part of the old city, for its architectural mix and majestic monuments

GUÉLIZ
Shops, cafés, eateries and nightclubs – it's all here in Marrakech at its most urbane

For a full description of each neighbourhood, see the Introduction.
Featured venues are colour-coded, according to the district in which they are located.